Ky's Blue Sky

A Special Needs Adventure

WRITTEN BY **Corie Frazier-Brown**

ILLUSTRATED BY **Wei Lu**

I would like to dedicate this book to my husband,
my beautiful mama, my amazing daddy whom I miss
dearly, my children and grandchildren, and
all the gardeners nurturing their seeds.

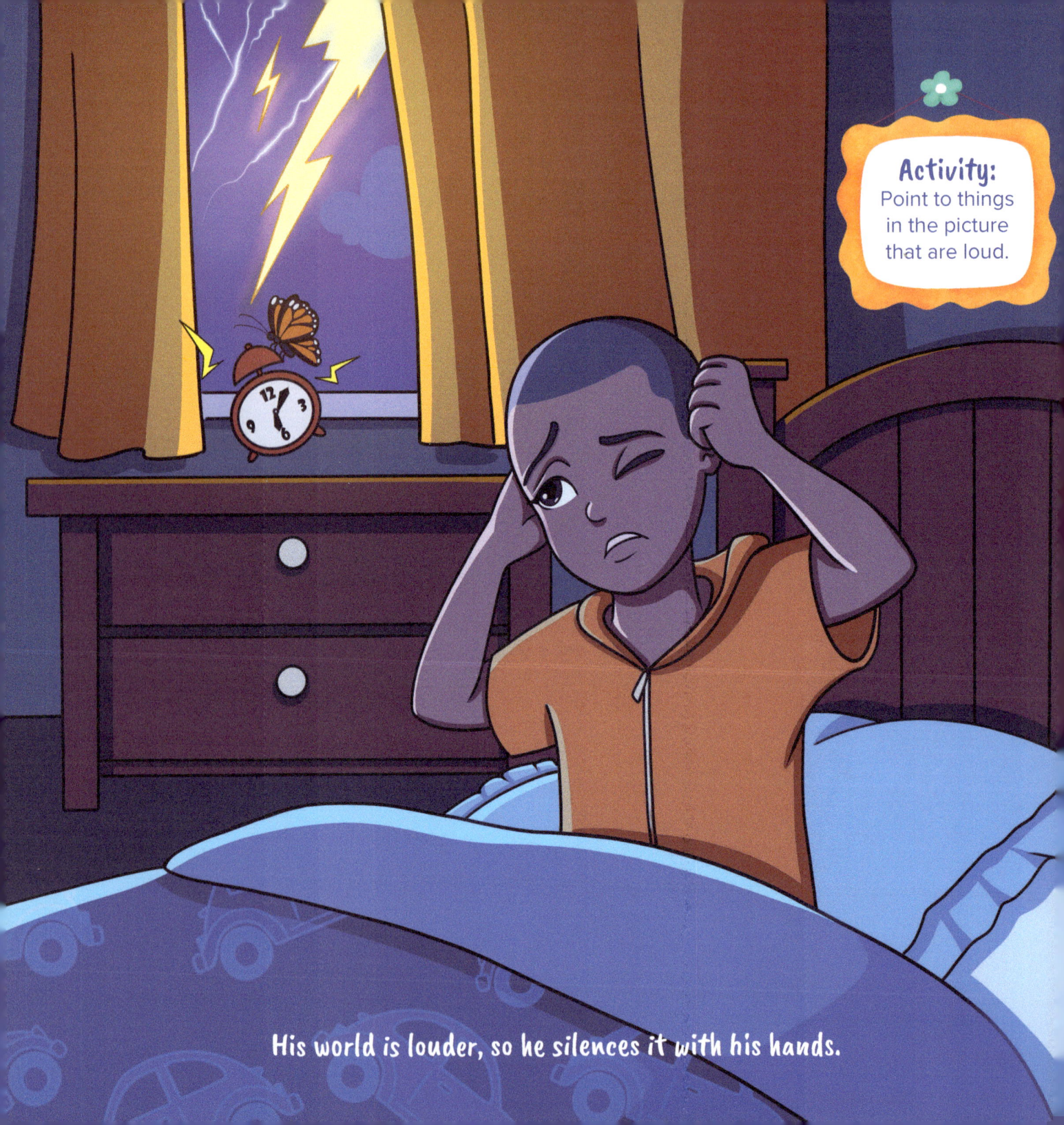

Activity:
Point to things in the picture that are loud.

His world is louder, so he silences it with his hands.

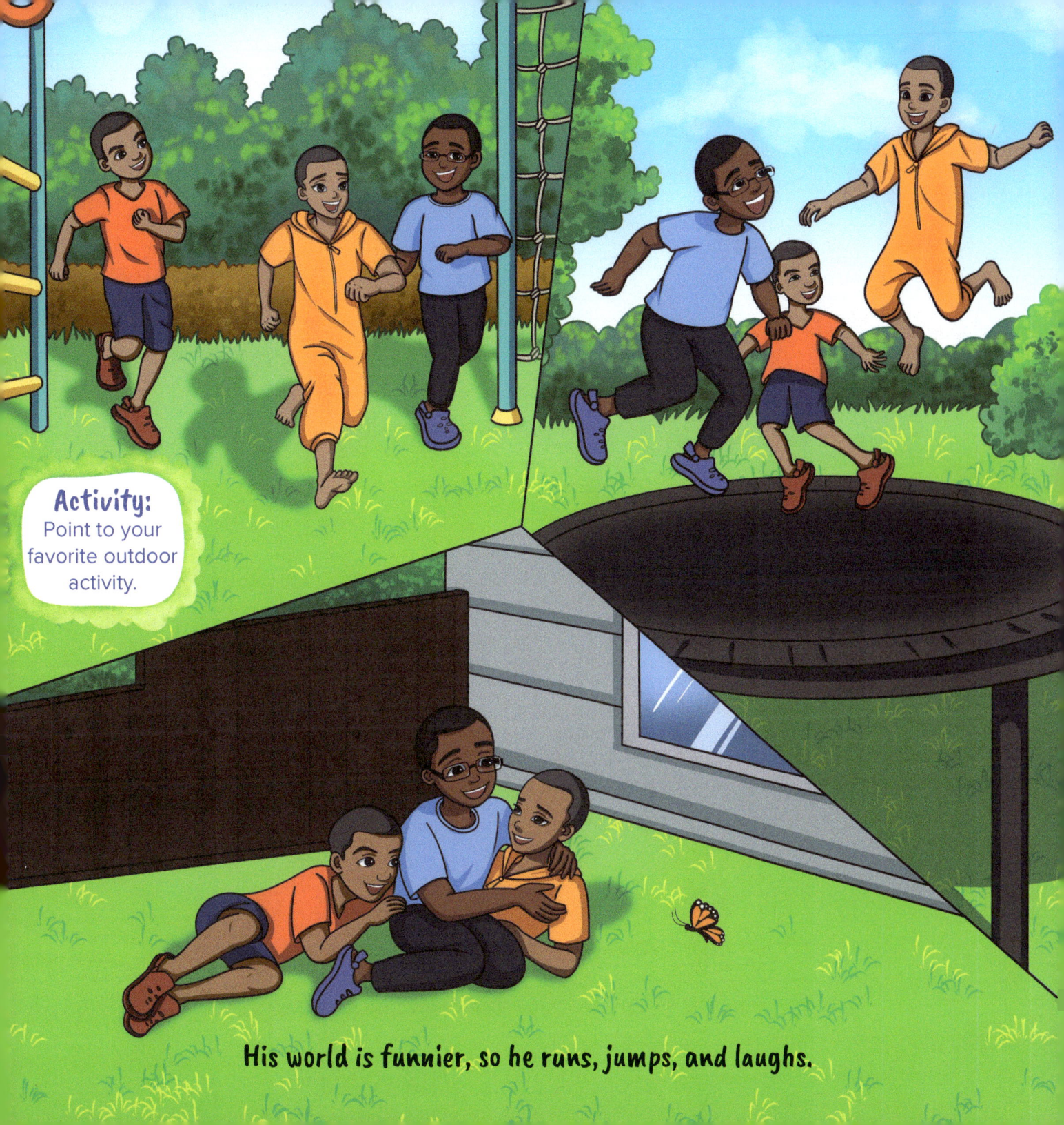

Activity:
Point to your favorite outdoor activity.

His world is funnier, so he runs, jumps, and laughs.

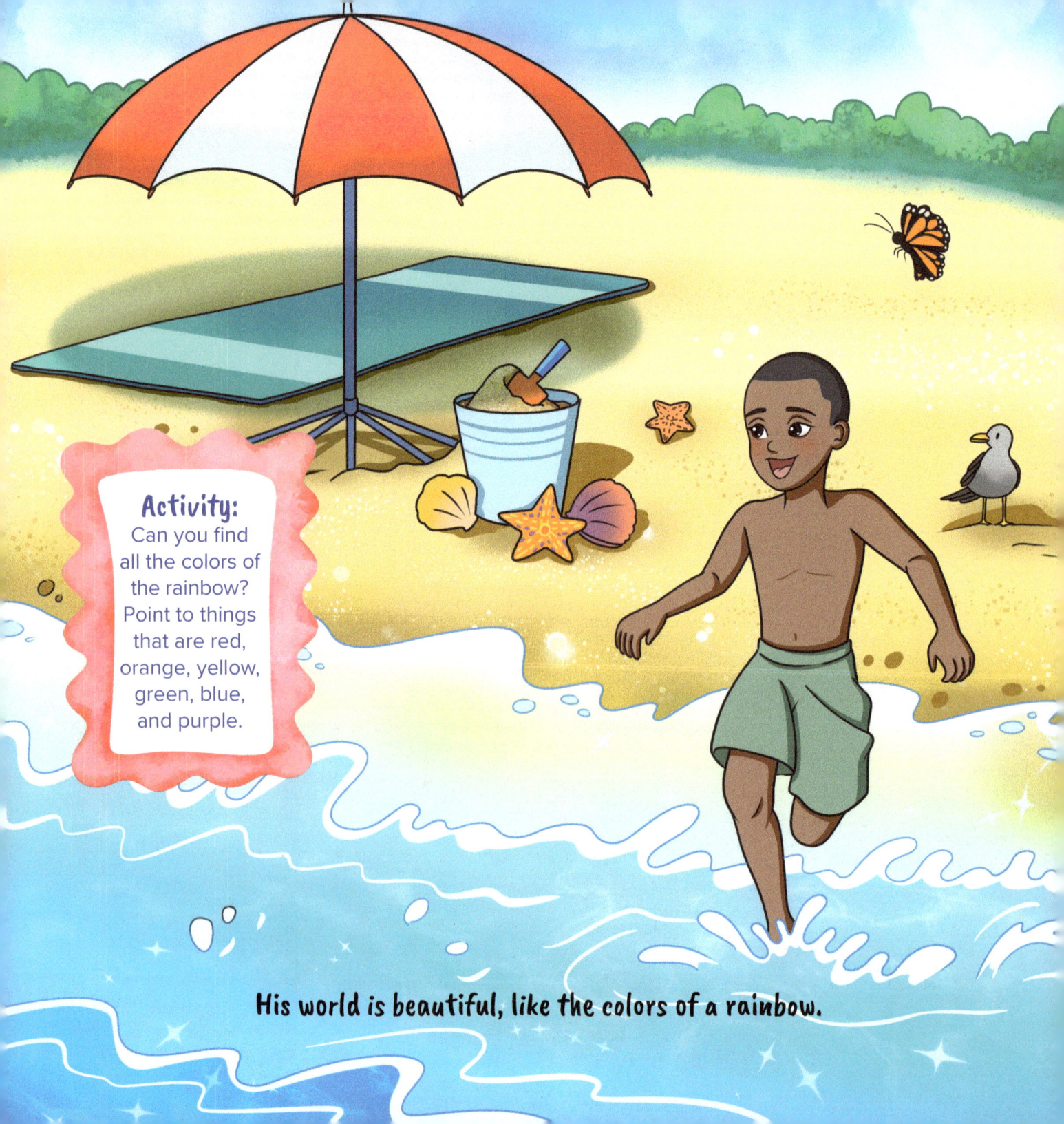

Activity:
Can you find all the colors of the rainbow? Point to things that are red, orange, yellow, green, blue, and purple.

His world is beautiful, like the colors of a rainbow.

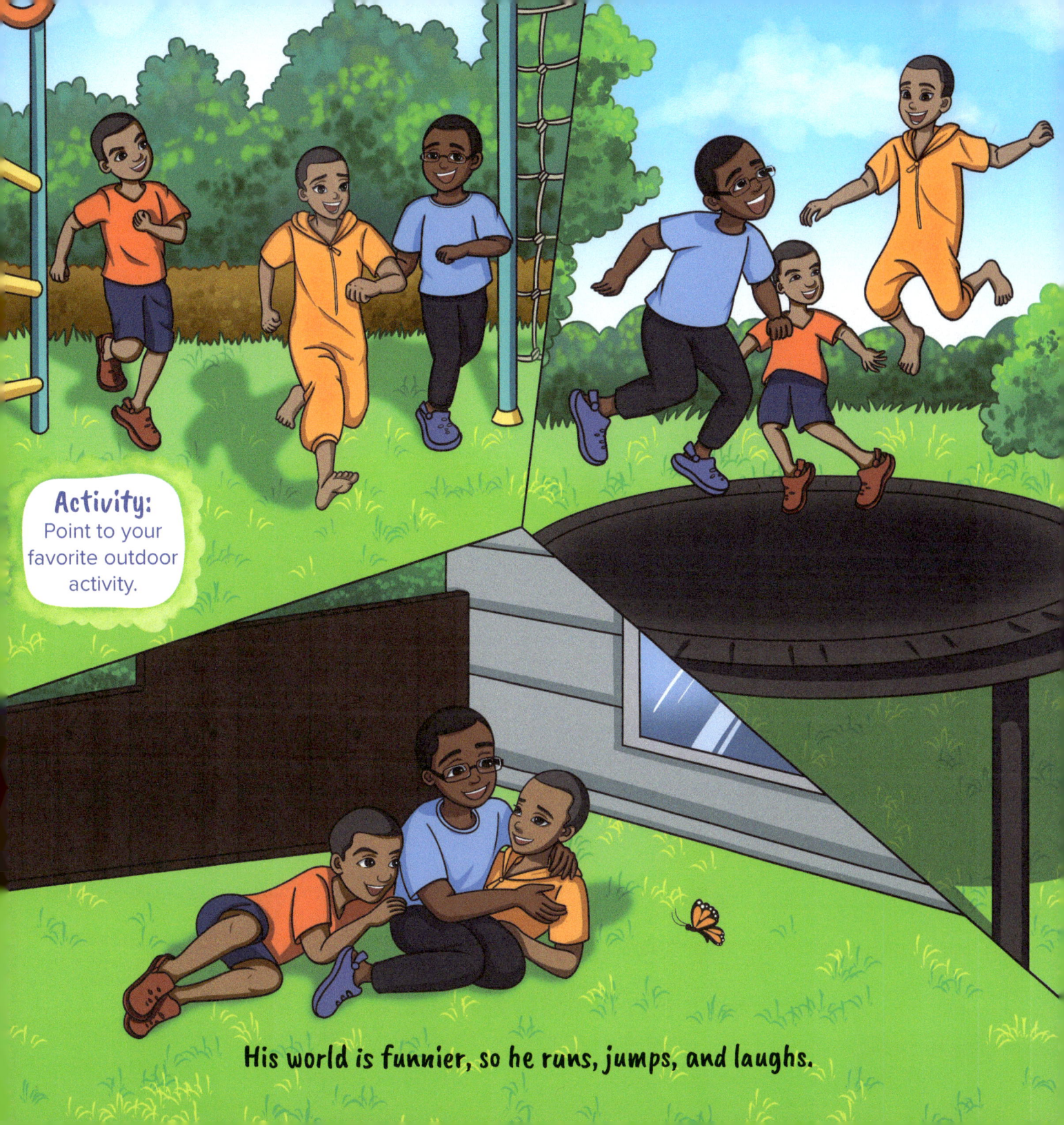

Activity:
Point to your favorite outdoor activity.

His world is funnier, so he runs, jumps, and laughs.

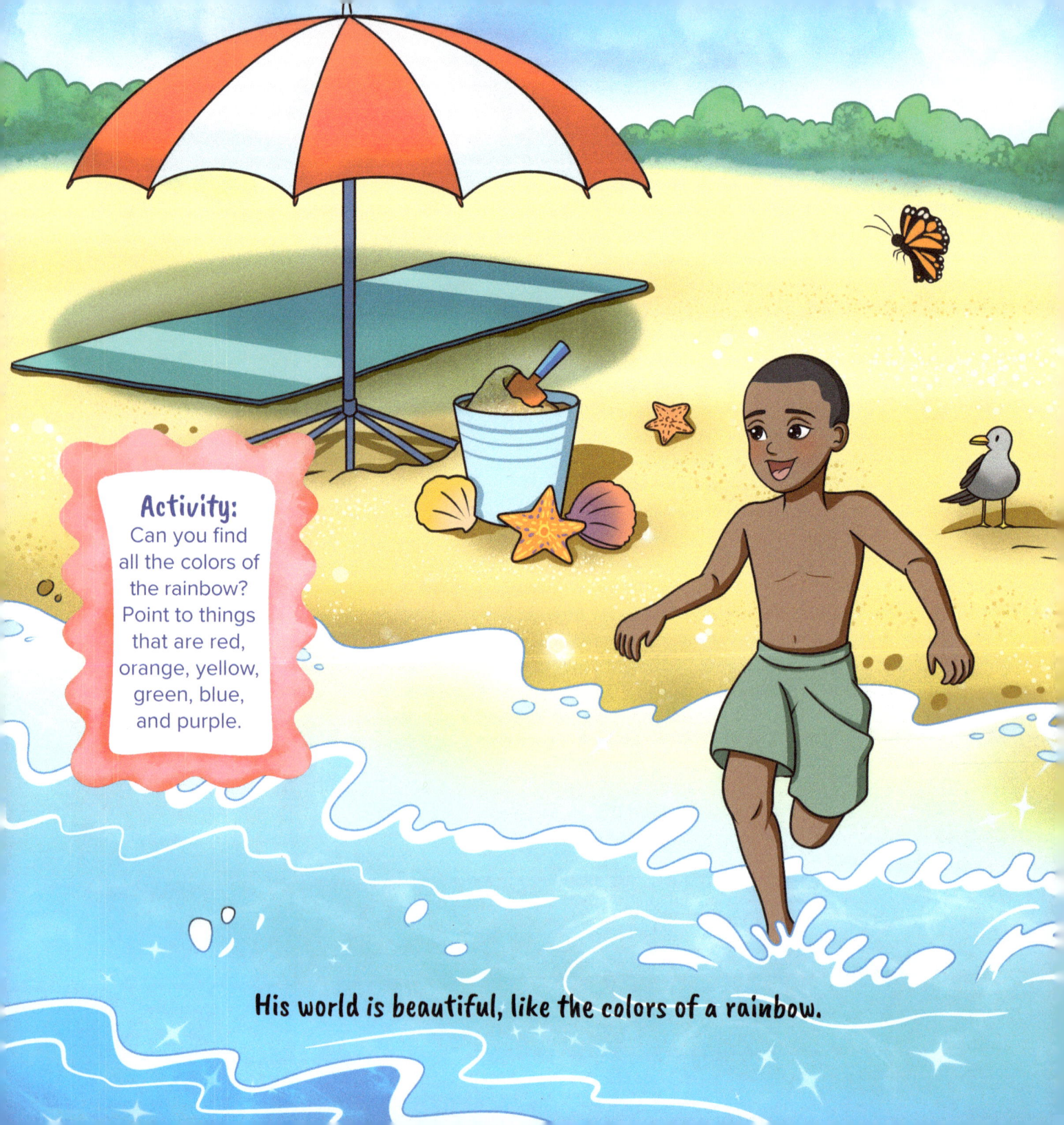

Activity:
Can you find all the colors of the rainbow? Point to things that are red, orange, yellow, green, blue, and purple.

His world is beautiful, like the colors of a rainbow.

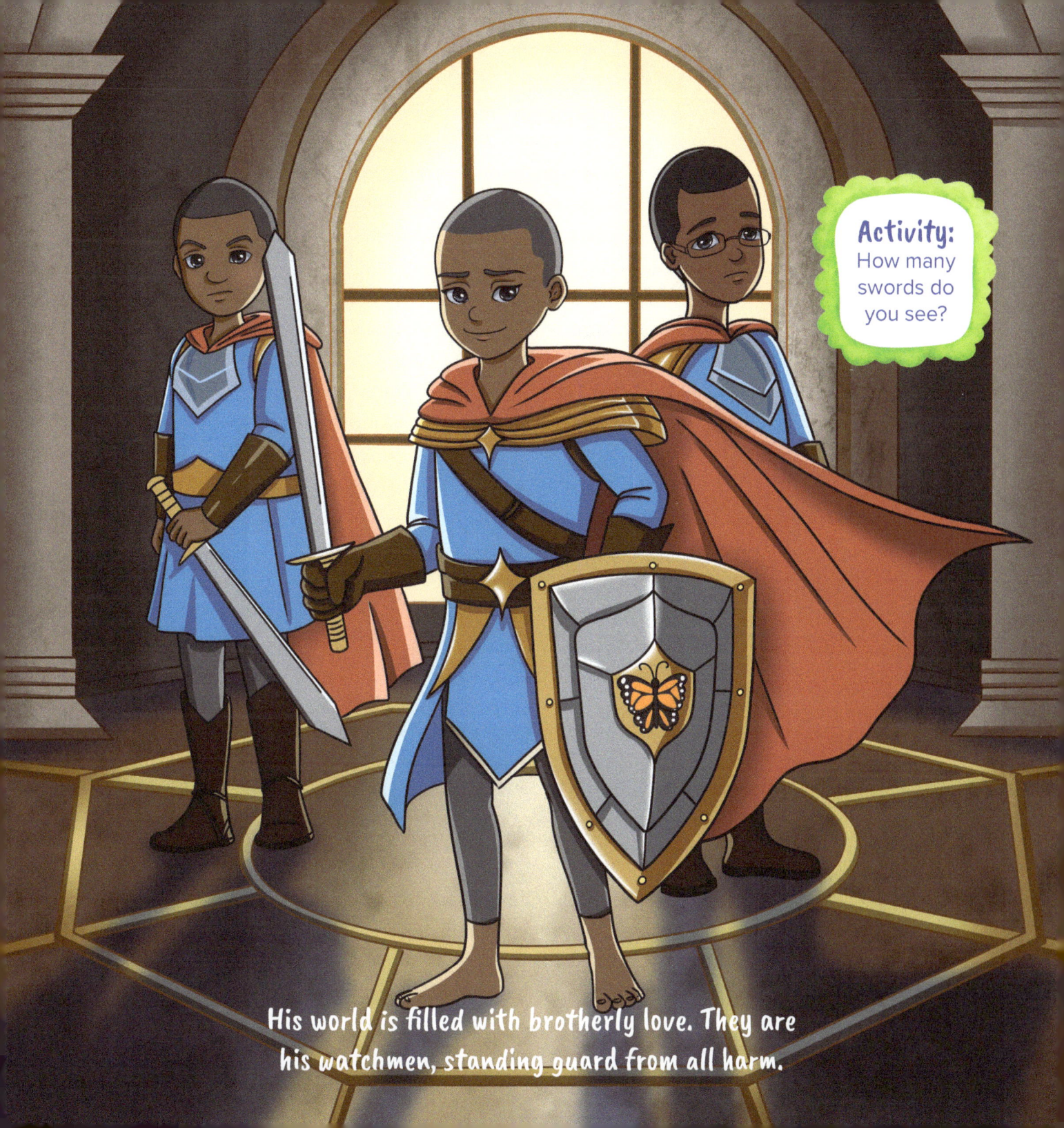

Activity: How many swords do you see?

His world is filled with brotherly love. They are his watchmen, standing guard from all harm.

His world is busy, spinning his toys around and around . . .

... while his eyes look for hidden treasures on the ground.

Activity:
Count the sticks, twigs, and flowers in the picture.

His world is filled with love and bear
hugs from the ones he loves . . .

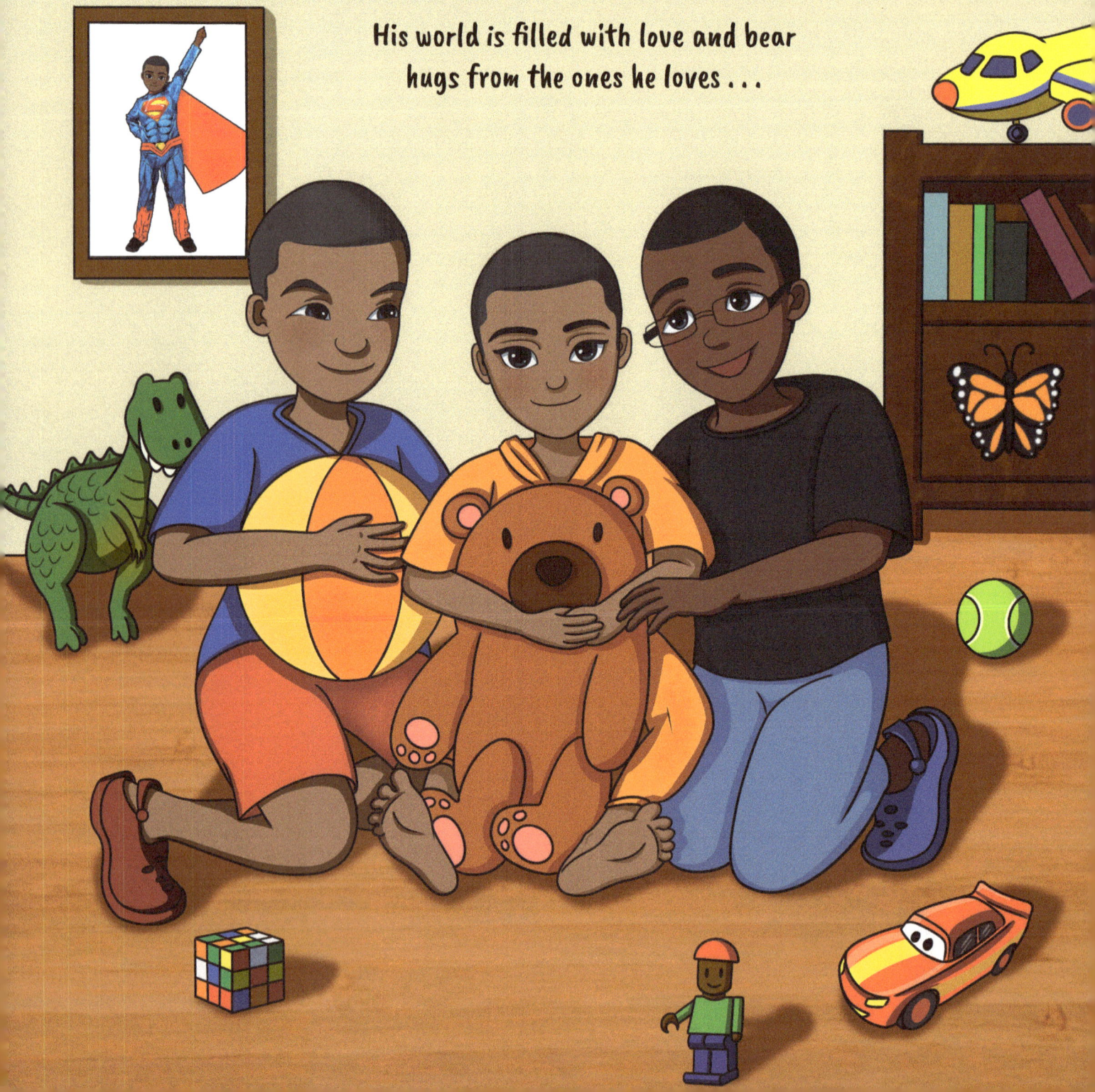

Activity:
Point to your
favorite
toy in the
pictures.

. . . and late nights spent making
snow angels while lying on the rug.

Activity:

Can you guess
why Ky is sad?

His world is sometimes filled
with unexplained tears.

But there's no need to cry,
little Ky, your family is always near.

His world is filled with challenges that many do not understand. But Ky continues to grow and thrive and do the best that he can.

His world is silent in an unperfect world,
but his eyes tell stories of blue skies and sunny days . . .
made by the Creator who fearfully
and wonderfully made him.

Activity:
Find all the yellow things on the page.

About the Author

Corie Frazier-Brown is a wife, mother of three adult children, and grandmother of four in South Carolina. She is passionate about her faith in God, walking in her divine purpose, and being an advocate for individuals on the spectrum. In her free time, Corie enjoys traveling, reading, writing, and spending time with her family.

About the Illustrator

Wei Lu is an internationally published illustrator whose work appears in novels, children's books, and branding. Wei attended NSCAD University's Interdisciplinary Design program, minored in illustration, and graduated with a bachelor of design.

"For I know the plans I have for you," declares the Lord, "plans to prosper you and not to harm you, plans to give you hope and a future."

Jeremiah 29:11

Milton Keynes UK
Ingram Content Group UK Ltd.
UKHW051718211124
451476UK00018BA/209

9 781961 065185